Smithsonian **kids**

STARS
AND THE
SOLAR
SYSTEM

Silver Dolphin

What Is Space?

When the Sun sets and the stars and Moon appear in the night sky, you are looking at a part of space. The universe, or all of space, is an incredibly huge, wide-open area that holds everything that can be measured or touched. Whether it's stars, galaxies, planets, or even you, they are all part of the universe.

The universe contains millions of galaxies. Galaxies are gigantic masses of gas, stars, dust, and dark matter, all held together by gravity. The stars that we can see from Earth are

all part of the Milky Way Galaxy. When the ancient Greeks looked up at the night sky, they noticed milky bands of light, so they named the galaxy the Milky Way.

Throughout history, humans have been fascinated by the mysteries of space and what was beyond Earth. It wasn't until 1961 that the first human was sent into space to orbit Earth. Today, space explorers and spacecraft continue to venture into space, searching for new discoveries and learning more about our galaxy and the universe.

We live in the Milky Way Galaxy, in one of the galaxy's spiral arms. We live in a solar system, a group of planets that orbit a star—in this case, that star is our Sun. Our solar system is made up of eight planets, plus moons, asteroids, comets, and more.

EARTH

Diameter	7,926 miles
Average Temperature	61°F
Year Length	365 days
Day Length	24 hours
Moons	1

SATURN

Diameter	74,898 miles
Average Temperature	-218°F
Year Length	10,759 days
Day Length	11 hours
Moons	82

URANUS

Diameter	31,763 miles
Average Temperature	-320°F
Year Length	30,687 days
Day Length	17 hours
Moons	27

Four of the planets are terrestrial, or solid with a rocky surface, and four of them are gas giants. The Sun is at the center of our solar system and is so big that its gravity causes everything in the solar system to orbit around it.

MARS

Diameter	4,220 miles
Average Temperature	-20°F
Year Length	687 days
Day Length	25 hours
Moons	2

MERCURY

Diameter	3,031 miles
Average Temperature	800°F during the day, -290°F at night
Year Length	88 days
Day Length	1,408 hours
Moons	0

JUPITER

Diameter	88,846 miles
Average Temperature	-162°F
Year Length	4,333 days
Day Length	10 hours
Moons	79

VENUS

Diameter	7,521 miles
Average Temperature	880°F
Year Length	225 days
Day Length	243 days
Moons	0

NEPTUNE

Diameter	30,775 miles
Average Temperature	-331°F
Year Length	60,190 days
Day Length	16 hours
Moons	14

Stars

From Earth, stars look like small, twinkling dots of light. But stars are not tiny, and they don't twinkle. Stars are enormous, hot balls of gas, mostly hydrogen and helium, that burn for millions or billions of years. Earth's closet star, the Sun, is 93 million miles away.

TYPES OF STARS

Stars are various colors because they burn at different temperatures. The hottest stars are white or blue, and cooler stars are orange or red. Stars can change color over time depending on their temperature.

DID YOU KNOW?

Stars don't really twinkle. Their light filters though Earth's atmosphere, scattering their steady glow, creating a twinkle effect.

Supergiants

Supergiants are the largest stars and give off a million times more energy than our Sun.

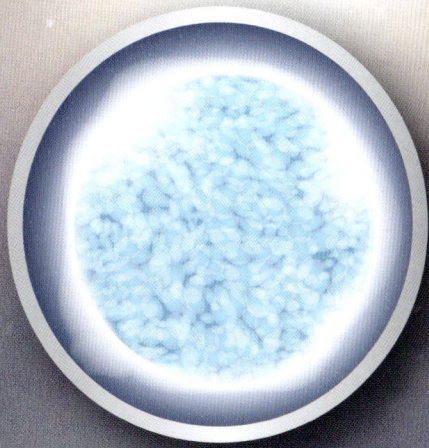

Blue Giants

Blue giants are the hottest stars and have a short life because they run out of fuel quickly.

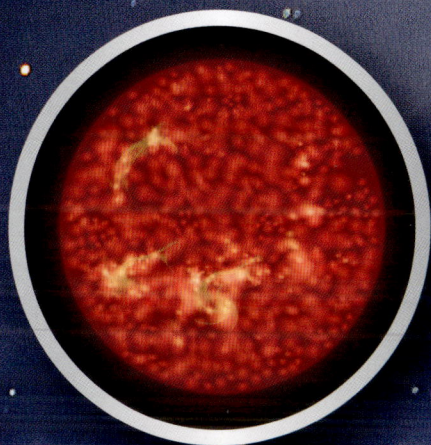

Red Giants

Red giants are cooler stars that are about thirty times larger than the Sun.

White Dwarfs

After a star has burned through all its nuclear fuel, it becomes a white dwarf. These are small, dense stars.

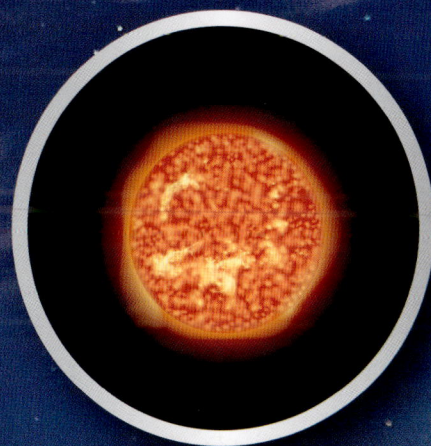

Red Dwarfs

Red dwarfs are small, cool stars. They glow very faintly—about a million times fainter than the Sun.

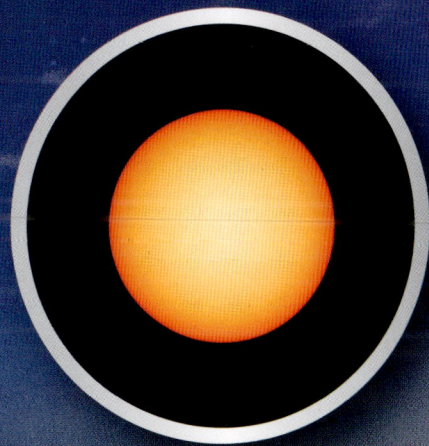

Yellow Dwarfs

These are medium-sized stars that live for about 10 billion years. Our Sun is a yellow dwarf star!

LIFE CYCLE OF STARS

All stars are born in a nebula, a huge cloud of gas and dust in space. Gravity pulls the gas and dust into a spinning ball called a protostar, or a young star. Stars the size of our Sun remain protostars for around 50 million years. The protostar gets hot enough to make its own energy, and then becomes a living star. Over time, stars burn through all their gases.

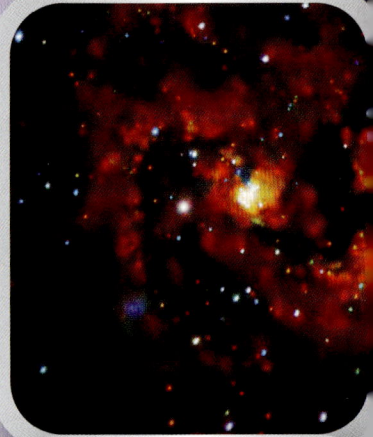

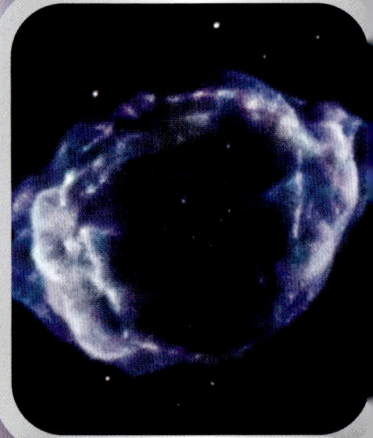

A star's life cycle ends depending on how big it is. Small stars grow bigger and brighter before they cool down, shrink, and die. Big stars get larger and hotter, and then they explode! The explosion, called a supernova, sends hot gases into space. On average, supernovas in the Milky Way occur about once every one hundred years.

DID YOU KNOW?

Everything in the universe (including us) was born from stars!

DEAD STARS

When stars die, they don't disappear—they change. When the atoms inside a star stop creating energy, the star is considered "dead." Medium-sized stars get bigger as they age until they turn into red giants. Eventually, they'll become white dwarfs surrounded by dust and gas.

Black Hole

When a large star dies, it sometimes creates a supernova. The dying star's middle collapses, and everything crushes together. Sometimes, a small, heavy neutron star forms. If the star keeps collapsing, a black hole is created. Gravity pulls things into a black hole. Nothing—not even light—can escape a black hole!

Except for our Sun, the stars we see in the sky are light-years away from Earth, meaning their light takes years to reach us. When you look up at the night sky, all the stars you can see are within the Milky Way Galaxy. There are trillions of stars beyond our galaxy that we can't see.

NAVIGATING BY THE STARS

Following patterns of stars in the sky helped people throughout history navigate, or find their way, on the sea. Later, scientists called astronomers made maps of the stars that anyone could follow. Today, boats have tools that help sailors find their way. But sailors still learn to read the stars in case their tools break! Astronauts learn to read star maps too.

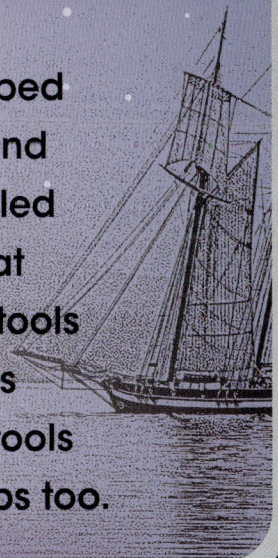

Our Shining Star: The Sun

The Sun is at the center of our solar system. Its light reaches Earth in eight minutes, and Earth's ideal distance from the Sun allows life to thrive on our planet. The Sun makes up 99.86 percent of our solar system's entire mass. It is 91 percent hydrogen and 8.9 percent helium. The last 0.1 percent is a mix of oxygen, carbon, nitrogen, silicon, and everything else that makes up the solar system. The planets, dwarf planets, asteroids, comets, meteoroids, and everything else in our solar system were all made from what was left over after the Sun formed.

The Sun has been burning for billions of years, and it'll continue burning for billions of years to come. Average-sized stars like the Sun usually burn for about 9 billion to 10 billion years. That means our Sun is about halfway through its life cycle. It will burn for about 5 billion more years. While the Sun may seem big to us, it's considered an average-sized star.

DID YOU KNOW?

The Sun is so big that 1 million Earths could fit inside it!

SUN

Diameter	864,000 miles
Average Temperature	10,000°F
Age	About 4.5 billion years

LAYERS OF THE SUN

CONVECTIVE ZONE

In the convective zone, huge bubbles of hot gas carry heat away from the Sun's center.

RADIATIVE ZONE

In the radiative zone, the energy created in the Sun's core is transferred outward.

CORE

All the Sun's energy is created in its core, the Sun's deepest zone.

CHROMOSPHERE

The chromosphere is the middle layer of the Sun's surface. Hydrogen in the chromosphere causes this layer to be red in color.

PHOTOSPHERE

The photosphere is the surface of the Sun. Darker areas on the Sun, called sunspots, can be found in the photosphere.

Famous Stars

Many of the brightest stars that we can see with the naked eye from Earth are well-known and are even named. You may have heard of the North Star (Polaris), but what about Rigel, Antares, or Sirius? Learn about these stars and more below. Then go outside tonight and see if you can spot them in the sky!

NORTH STAR

The North Star, or Polaris, is not the brightest star in the sky, but it's one of the easiest to find in the Northern Hemisphere. The North Star is located directly above Earth's North Pole. Throughout history, people have used the North Star to navigate. If one is ever lost, they can just look to the North Star and know they're facing north.

BETELGEUSE

Betelgeuse is a red supergiant star that appears more orange than other stars in the sky. Betelgeuse is located at the shoulder of the constellation Orion. Betelgeuse is nearing the end of its life and will explode in a supernova within the next 100,000 years. The supernova will be so bright it will be seen during daytime!

SIRIUS

Sirius is one of the brightest stars in the sky. And it's not alone. Sirius is a binary star, meaning that it is accompanied by a small white dwarf star that's smaller than Earth.

ARCTURUS

In the Northern Hemisphere, Arcturus is visible most days of the year. This red giant is one of the brightest stars in the sky and is twenty-five times larger than the Sun.

RIGEL

Rigel is also located in the constellation Orion, at the point of his left foot. This blue supergiant is located 860 light-years from Earth, which means how we see Rigel today is what it looked like 860 years ago!

ANTARES

Antares is a red supergiant star that appears in the constellation Scorpius. Because of its orange hue, Antares is often mistaken for the planet Mars, which can also be seen without a telescope. In fact, the name Antares means "rival to Ares." Ares is the Greek name for Mars.

DID YOU KNOW?

When you wish upon a falling star, you're really wishing upon a meteor! Meteors are pieces of rock and metal that heat up and glow when they enter Earth's atmosphere.

Telescopes and Seeing Stars

Astronomers are scientists who study everything beyond Earth. Some use instruments to make direct observations, while others use theories to investigate topics that cannot be directly seen. Though ancient people recorded stars, constellations, and night-sky observations for thousands of years, modern astronomy began in 1608 when the telescope was invented.

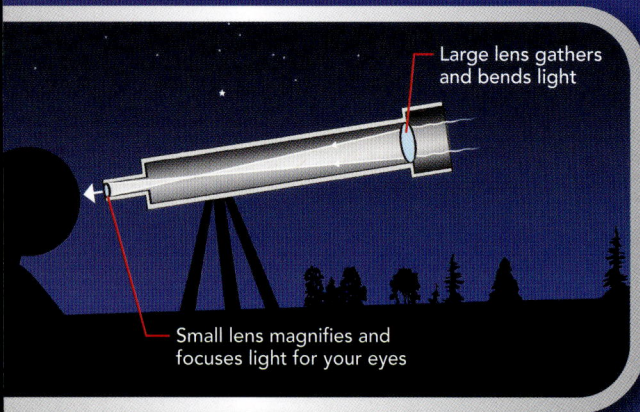

Large lens gathers and bends light

Small lens magnifies and focuses light for your eyes

TELESCOPES

The first telescope was a long tube with a lens inside, like an eyeglass. The inventor of the first telescope, Hans Lippershey, also made eyeglasses. Some telescopes still use lenses. Light bends as it passes through the lenses. Other telescopes use curved mirrors, where light bounces from one mirror to another. Lenses and mirrors make faraway objects look closer. They make blurry objects look clear.

In 1609, astronomer Galileo Galilei was the first person to use a telescope to study space. Telescopes have changed a lot since then. Some telescopes can see space objects in faraway galaxies! Today, astronomy is often done with the help of computers instead of directly looking through telescopes.

OBSERVATORIES

Observatories are buildings that house telescopes and other equipment that are used to view and study space. Observatories around the world study different things; some examine objects outside the solar system such as stars or galaxies, while others look at the Sun and its atmosphere. Observatories on Earth are often located on remote mountaintops where there is less light pollution from cities that interfere with viewing space. Some observatories even orbit Earth in space.

THE HUBBLE TELESCOPE

The size of a school bus, the orbiting Hubble Telescope was launched into space by the National Aeronautics and Space Administration (NASA) on April 24, 1990. Since its launch, scientists have used the Hubble to gather information about our solar system, distant stars and galaxies, and much more.

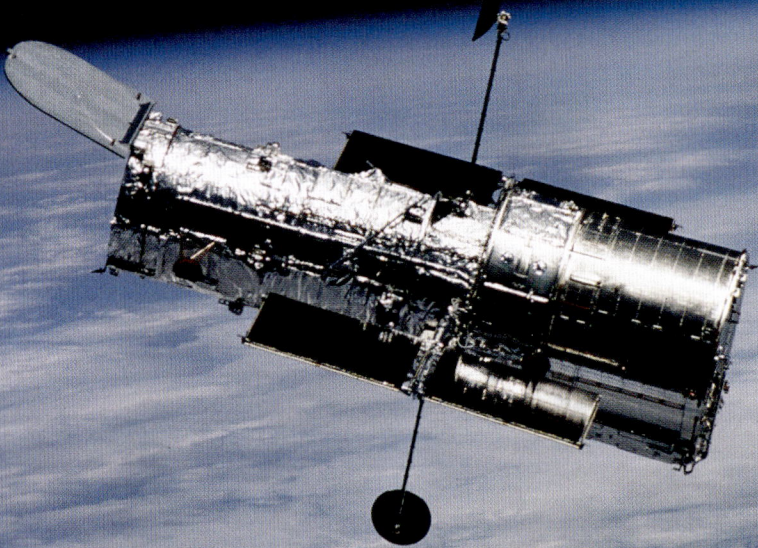

The Hubble orbits 340 miles above Earth and travels five miles per second. At that speed, the Hubble could travel across the United States in ten minutes. Because the Hubble faces away from Earth's atmosphere, which can blur and distort images, its technology can study space better than telescopes on Earth can.

Since its launch, the Hubble has traveled 4 billion miles in Earth's orbit. It has made over 1.5 million observations, and has taken pictures of planets, black holes, comets, distant galaxies, dying stars, and more.

JAMES WEBB SPACE TELESCOPE

The James Webb Space Telescope is an orbiting observatory telescope that launched in December 2021 to expand on the knowledge the Hubble Telescope has gained.

The James Webb Space Telescope is the largest telescope ever launched into space. Its sun shield, which protects it from light and heat, is as large as a tennis court! About one hundred times more powerful than the Hubble, the James Webb Space Telescope's technology is so advanced that it can study light that was emitted 13.5 billion years ago. It's able to view objects from the distant past in so much detail because of its longer visible wavelengths and its large primary mirror.

Unlike the Hubble, the James Webb Space Telescope will orbit the Sun instead of Earth. Scientists hope that the James Webb Space Telescope will discover more about supermassive black holes and how they develop in galaxies, among other scientific questions.

DID YOU KNOW?

The James Webb Space Telescope can see the details on a penny from about twenty-four miles away.

What Are Constellations?

For as long as humans have existed, they have looked up at the stars. They imagined connecting lines between the stars, like a giant dot-to-dot puzzle, to create pictures in the sky. These pictures, called constellations, were of animals or people. Ancient peoples created stories and myths around the constellations. Cultures around the world have identified and named different sets of constellations, but only eighty-eight are considered official by the International Astronomical Union (IAU).

The eighty-eight official constellations are mostly based on Greek mythology, and about forty-two of the official constellations are named for animals. More than half of the constellations can be seen from the Northern Hemisphere. The rest are visible only from below Earth's equator, in the Southern Hemisphere. Constellations are not always found in the exact same location in the sky.

As Earth revolves around the Sun, the constellations' locations in the sky vary throughout the year. Although the stars in constellations may look close to one another, they are hundreds or thousands of light-years apart.

Thousands of years ago, ancient people depicted constellations on cave walls.

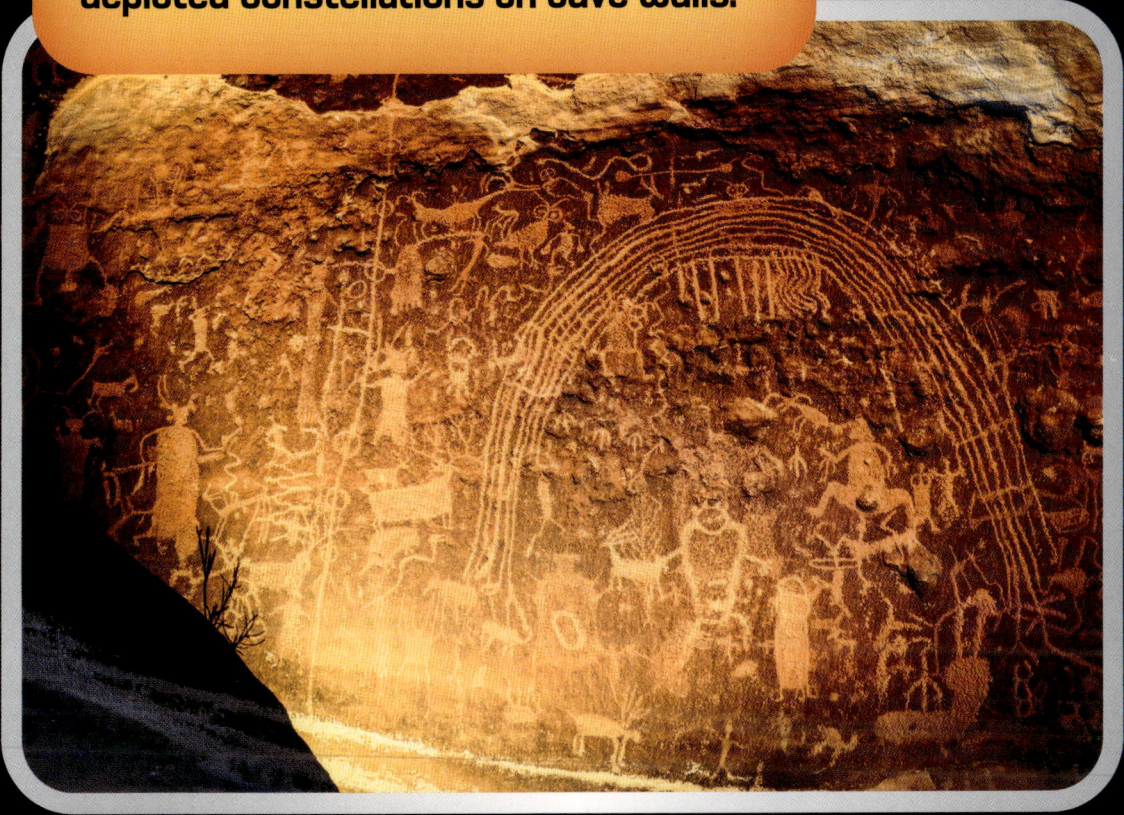

There are many recognizable constellations in the night sky, such as Ursa Major and Orion. However, throughout history, different cultures viewed constellations in their own way.

For example, the constellation we call Scorpius (scorpion) looked like a magical fishhook to ancient Polynesians. While we view the constellation Capricornus as a goat, the ancient Aztecs called it Cipactli, or "whale."

Capricornus

The Western Zodiac Constellations

The zodiac is a group of twelve constellations through which the Sun, Moon, and planets appear to pass by in one year. Ancient people used the zodiac to track the seasons. They noticed that the Sun appeared to pass through one of the constellations about once a month. Today, we use this same theory to assign dates to each zodiac sign. You may have heard the question "What's your sign?"; this means that your birthday falls within a zodiac sign's time frame. Use the chart below to figure out your zodiac sign!

CAPRICORNUS (goat): December 22–January 19

AQUARIUS (water bearer): January 20–February 18

PISCES (fish): February 19–March 20

ARIES (ram): March 21–April 19

TAURUS (bull): April 20–May 20

GEMINI (twins): May 21–June 21

CANCER (crab): June 22–July 22

LEO (lion): July 23–August 22

VIRGO (virgin): August 23–September 22

LIBRA (scales): September 23–October 23

SCORPIUS (scorpion): October 24–November 21

SAGITTARIUS (archer): November 22–December 21

Try This!
What is your zodiac sign? Use the included glow-in-the-dark stars to create your very own zodiac constellation on your wall!

The zodiac constellations we follow today align with what people saw 2,000 years ago. Because Earth's axis has shifted over time, the constellations today are not in the same position as they were thousands of years ago.

If the constellations were mapped today, they'd be about a month different from the original constellation mapping.

CAPRICORNUS
(DECEMBER 22–JANUARY 19)

Capricornus is a constellation depicting a goat with the tail of a fish. It is believed that this is one of the oldest recorded constellations— this constellation was documented over 4,000 years ago by the Babylonians.

AQUARIUS
(JANUARY 20–FEBRUARY 18)

Aquarius is a constellation meaning "water bearer" and depicts a man pouring water out of a cup. It is located in an area of the sky known as the "sea" because many constellations that have water themes are located in this stretch of sky.

PISCES
(FEBRUARY 19–MARCH 20)

Pisces, or "fish," is also located in the "sea" of the sky. This constellation depicts two fish that are connected to each other by a line or ribbon. One of the fish features a circlet, or ring of seven stars.

ARIES
(MARCH 21–APRIL 19)

Located in the Northern Hemisphere, Aries is Latin for "ram." A star called Hamal is one of the brightest stars in this constellation. Hamal is Arabic for "lamb."

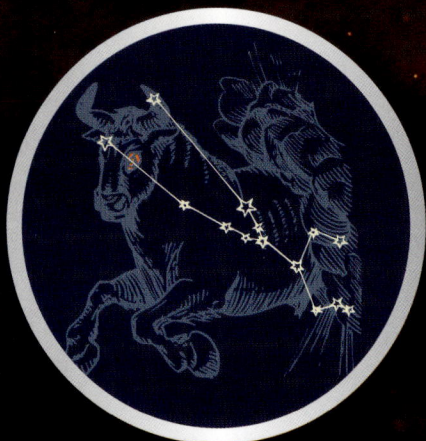

TAURUS
(APRIL 20–MAY 20)

Taurus is a constellation depicting a bull. Its V shape represents the bull's head. The star called Aldebaran is the brightest star in the constellation, and it symbolizes the bull's glowing orange eye.

GEMINI
(MAY 21–JUNE 21)

Gemini is a constellation that shows twins. The twins are viewed differently depending on the culture. In ancient Egypt, the twins were viewed as twin goats. In Arabian astronomy, they were seen as twin peacocks. In most Western cultures, the twins are named after gods Castor and Pollux from Greek mythology.

CANCER
(JUNE 22–JULY 22)

The cancer constellation represents a crab. In Greek mythology, a crab bit the foot of the god Hercules while he was fighting a multiheaded snake. This constellation features a cluster of stars called the Beehive.

LEO
(JULY 23–AUGUST 22)

Leo is a constellation that depicts a lion. This constellation can be seen from anywhere on Earth except Antarctica. One of the brightest stars in the sky, Regulus, is located in Leo. Regulus is Arabic for "heart of the lion."

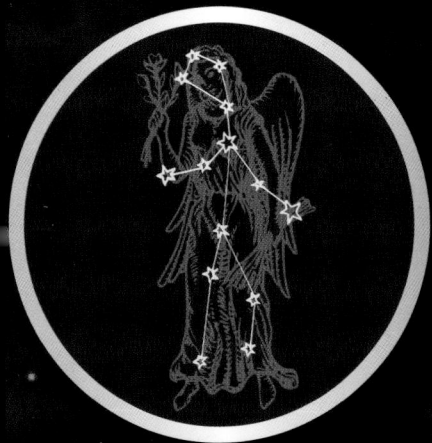

VIRGO
(AUGUST 23–SEPTEMBER 22)

Virgo is a constellation that depicts a maiden holding a bundle of wheat and is viewed as a goddess of harvest. As one of the largest constellations in the night sky, just one part of it includes 1,300 galaxies located 55 million light-years away.

LIBRA
(SEPTEMBER 23–OCTOBER 23)

Libra is a constellation depicting scales and represents the concept of balance. Virgo, the neighboring constellation, can also be viewed as holding the scales.

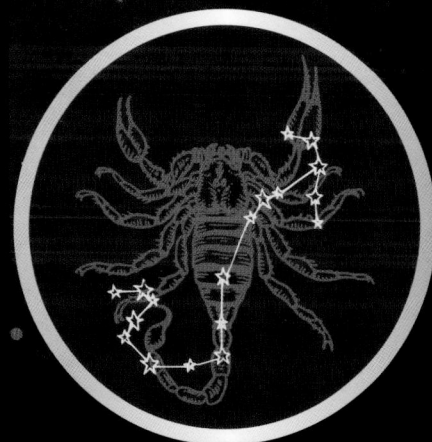

SCORPIUS
(OCTOBER 24–NOVEMBER 21)

Scorpius, or "scorpion," is one of the most recognizable constellations in the sky. According to Greek myth, the goddess Artemis sent a scorpion to kill the hunter Orion. Because the scorpion and Orion were enemies, these two constellations never appear in the sky at the same time.

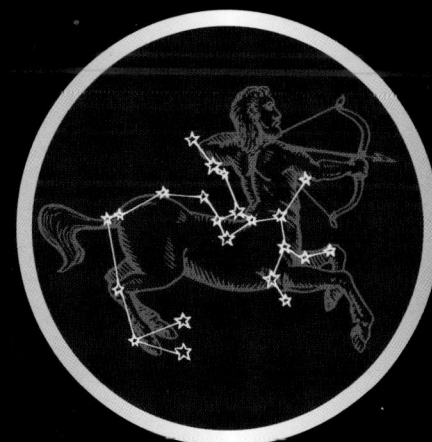

SAGITTARIUS
(NOVEMBER 22–DECEMBER 21)

Sagittarius is a constellation depicting a centaur (half man, half horse) as an archer, drawing his bow. A smaller group of stars in this constellation is called the Teapot.

Famous Constellations: Orion

Orion is one of the most famous constellations. It is named after the Greek god of hunting. The three bright stars in a row are Orion's belt. According to myth, Orion bragged about how great he was at hunting. Gaia, Greek goddess of Earth, sent a scorpion to stop him from hunting. Orion was stung by the scorpion and placed in the sky as a constellation.

To see Orion, look to the southwestern sky in the Northern Hemisphere and the northwestern sky in the Southern Hemisphere and look for three stars in a row to spot his belt. Orion can be viewed from November to February.

To create your very own Orion in your room, grab twenty of your included stars and follow the picture below.

Orion

Some of the most recognizable constellations in the night sky are Ursa Major and Ursa Minor. Their names mean "big bear" and "little bear." According to myth, the Greek god Zeus turned a mother and son into bears, then threw them by their tails into the night sky to protect them from Zeus's wife, Hera. Ursa Major is the mother bear.

The bear's tail forms the handle of the Big Dipper, a group of seven stars in a spoonlike shape.

Ursa Minor is known as the Little Dipper. At the end of the bear's tail is the constellation's brightest star: Polaris, or the North Star. The North Star is always north of where one is standing, so it works like a compass. Ursa Major and Ursa Minor are always visible on clear nights from Earth's Northern Hemisphere—the top half of the globe.

Ursa Major

To create Ursa Major, use seven of the included stars and follow the picture to the right.

To create Ursa Minor, use seven of the included stars and follow the picture to the right.

Ursa Minor

Famous Constellations: Cassiopeia

According to Greek mythology, Cassiopeia was a vain queen. Though her constellation consists of stars that create a W shape, sometimes the larger image around the constellation is viewed as a woman sitting in a chair combing her hair.

To create Cassiopeia, use five of the included stars and follow the picture below.

Cassiopeia

Famous Constellations: Hydra

Hydra is a constellation depicting a water snake. According to Greek mythology, Hydra was a monster with many heads that the god Hercules fought. It is the longest constellation in the sky—wrapping more than a quarter of the way across the sky.

To create Hydra, use twenty of the included stars and follow the picture below.

Hydra

Stellar Night Sky

On Earth, our closest star, the Sun, keeps us warm and gives us light, allows plants and food to grow, and creates our weather. Without it, life on Earth wouldn't be possible. Every night, after the Sun sets, we're able to view hundreds of more stars. And though all stars eventually die, over time the leftovers of stars combine with gas and dust. New stars are created, and the galaxy lives on.

When you're finished creating constellations and starry skies in your room with the included glow-in-the-dark stars, go outside at night and look up. The stars you see are what they looked like hundreds or thousands of years ago. And while they look like tiny specks of light, many are hundreds of times bigger than our Sun. We are still learning so much about the stars in our galaxy and beyond.

A great way to start learning is to just get outside and observe the vast starry sky. What can you see tonight?